Let's Be Real About the Single Life

Workbook

NATHANIEL HOLLOWAY

Copyright © 2014 Nathaniel Holloway

All rights reserved.

ISBN-13:978-1499723786
ISBN-10:1499723784

CONTENTS

Overview

Singleness at a Glance

Things that Influence Your Singleness

Myths about Being Single

The Benefits of Being Single

The Negative Effects

Understanding the Purpose of Being Single

Temptation: Your Worst Enemy

"Let's Talk about Sex!"

Dealing with Loneliness

Dating

The 10 Commandments of Dating

Building a Successful Relationship

"Are You Ready for Marriage?"

Overview

Welcome

This workbook is really about helping you learn how to live more fruitfully, more effectively, and more abundantly as a single Christian and Christian couples. That's why I've designed it as a hands-on process. When you participate in your own learning process, you'll have a greater understanding of how to live a fulfilling life.

Getting Started

This workbook is for those who want to see significant change in their lives in the areas of singleness and relationships. I'm confident that you will not just be taught, but you will be transformed in the process.

Singleness is the time of less demand in your life. It's the period of life that you focus on your relationship with God, allowing Him to form your character into the person He called you to be. It's also the period in your life where you discipline yourself to become a whole person before you get married.

In this workbook you will be introduced to powerful tools and techniques to create a successful single lifestyle and relationships. Coupled with the book, Let's Be Real about the Single Life, this workbook provides powerful insight that will move your single life and relationships forward. You are going to see your world of relationships and as a single Christian from a new perspective.

Let's Be Real about the Single Life

SINGLENESS AT A GLANCE

Let's Talk

What do you expect will be your biggest challenge(s) as you begin this journey?

_____
_____
_____
_____
_____
_____
_____
_____
_____
_____
_____
_____
_____
_____
_____
_____
_____
_____
_____
_____

Singleness at a glance

There are many factors that contribute to how you view being single. Some are good and some are bad. In this session we're going to take a look at the three main contributors that impact your view of singleness.

One of the biggest deceptions in society today is that you have to be in a relationship or married in order to be happy, which is so far from the truth. The radio is filled with songs talking about loving someone all night long, and the television shows are filled with scenes of soft porn. Talk about trying to keep your eye and ear gates pure! Many singles feel pressured to be in a relationship or married by a certain age.

Question

How do you feel about being single?

_____
_____
_____
_____
_____
_____

Do you feel you can't be happy without a relationship? Why?

_____
_____
_____
_____
_____
_____

Do you feel that everything would be just fine if you could find that one special person?

_____
_____
_____
_____
_____
_____

Does being single make you think negative thoughts about yourself?

_____
_____
_____
_____
_____
_____

What is it about being single that makes you feel bad?

_____
_____
_____
_____
_____
_____

Are you ashamed of being single? Why?

_____
_____
_____
_____

_____
_____

Are you in control of your singleness, or is your singleness in control of you?

_____
_____
_____
_____
_____
_____

THINGS THAT INFLUENCE YOUR SINGLENESS

Let's Talk

How has your singleness been influenced?

Things That Influence Your Singleness

Influence is the application of power to accomplish a specific purpose. Every time you try to affect how other people think, behave or make decisions, you are trying to influence them. There are many things that can have an influence on your single life if you allow them to. Some positive, some negative.

Questions

What are some things that have or continue to influence how you feel about being single?

_____
_____
_____
_____
_____

How do your friends influence the way you feel about being single?

_____
_____
_____
_____
_____

How does what you watch on television and the music you listen to influence the way you feel about being single?

_____
_____
_____
_____
_____
_____

How does your surroundings influence the way you feel about being single?

_____
_____
_____
_____
_____
_____

MYTHS ABOUT BEING SINGLE

Let's Talk

What myths about being single have you heard? How have they impacted your life?

___

Myths About Being Single

I found that there are lots myths about being single. Because of the way society portrays the single life, for many single Christians, it's easy to believe those myths. Myths about being single will only cause you to pursue relationships for all the wrong reasons. Let's take a look at some common myths I discovered about being single.

Questions

What single myths do you believe? Why?

_____
_____
_____
_____
_____
_____

Do you feel that you are lonely because you are single? Why?

_____
_____
_____
_____
_____
_____

Do you feel that all of your problems can be solve by being in a relationship? Why?

_____
_____
_____

_____
_____
_____

Do you feel that something is wrong with you because you are single? Why?

_____
_____
_____
_____
_____
_____

THE BENEFITS OF BEING SINGLE

Let's Talk

What do you feel have been some benefits in your singleness?

_____
_____
_____
_____
_____
_____
_____
_____
_____
_____
_____
_____
_____
_____
_____
_____
_____
_____
_____
_____

The Benefits of Singleness

When you seriously think about it, there are actually benefits to being single. It's easy to say that there are no advantages if all we see are the negative aspects.

Questions

Do you have total freedom in your singleness right now?

_____
_____
_____
_____
_____
_____

What are you doing to maximize your freedom?

_____
_____
_____
_____
_____
_____

Do you have control of your emotions? If no, why not?

_____
_____
_____
_____
_____
_____

Do you have control of your money? If no, why not?

_____
_____
_____
_____
_____

Let's Be Real about the Single Life

THE NEGATIVE EFFECTS

Let's Talk

How has being single affected you negatively?

_____

The Negative Effects

When dealing with being single, if you continue to allow it to be a problem, it can and will destroy you. It starts out as just a little thought, and then it gets bigger and bigger, until it consumes you. For example, there was a period in my life when I made the decision to stop having sex and live totally for God. I did it for four years straight, and then one day I fell.

When I got back on the right track, it got so hard to keep that door closed was I allowed it to be opened again. It felt like the pull was seven times stronger.

Questions

Are you obsessed with the idea of being in a relationship? Why?

_____
_____
_____
_____
_____
_____

Are you making any wrong decisions?

_____
_____
_____
_____
_____
_____

How have your wrong decisions affected you?

_____
_____
_____
_____
_____
_____

Are you settling for less than you deserve? Why?

_____
_____
_____
_____
_____
_____

UNDERSTANDING THE PURPOSE OF BEING SINGLE

Let's Talk

What is your purpose?

Understanding The Purpose of Being Single

The number one problem I've found with many single Christians today is that they don't fully understand the purpose of them being single. Many were never told that there even was a purpose for being single. There is a purpose for every period in your life. Everything we go through and every period in our life has a purpose, a deliberate plan a proposition, an advance plan, and an intention, a design.

Question

To you, what does it mean to be single and what scripture supports your answer?

_____
_____
_____
_____
_____
_____

What is the content of your character?

_____
_____
_____
_____
_____
_____

What do you feel your purpose is?

_____
_____
_____
_____
_____
_____

What are you doing to fulfill your purpose?

_____
_____
_____
_____
_____
_____

Let's Be Real about the Single Life

TEMPTATION

Let's Talk

How does temptation impact your life?

_____
_____
_____
_____
_____
_____
_____
_____
_____
_____
_____
_____
_____
_____
_____
_____
_____
_____
_____

Temptation (Your Worst Enemy!)

When you think of temptation you probably think of it as sexual, many singles do. But it's more to it than just sex. It's a process of elevation. "You're probably thinking to yourself, huh?" or asking yourself, "How is it a process of elevation?" Answering the following questions will give you a better understanding.

Questions

What is temptation to you?

_____
_____
_____
_____
_____
_____

What are the things that tempt you to sin? Is it something that you are always thinking about?

_____
_____
_____
_____
_____
_____

What are some things that trigger your temptations?

_____
_____
_____
_____
_____

Do you have true patience? Explain.

_____
_____
_____
_____
_____

How do you handle temptations when they come?

_____
_____
_____
_____
_____

When you try to deal with your temptations on your own, what is the outcome? What is the outcome when you seek God?

_____
_____
_____
_____
_____

What steps are you taking toward your victory?

_____
_____
_____
_____
_____
_____

Let's Be Real about the Single Life

LET'S TALK ABOUT SEX

Let's Talk

What is your view on sex?

_____

Let's Talk About Sex

The biggest issue singles deal with is sex. Especially when you've had it before. Sex is a biological drive oriented toward pleasure and often procreation. I feel that it's bigger than drugs or alcohol. Satan knows that you can stop drinking or smoking at will. You can control when you are around drugs, but sex is presented to you from every angle. Whether through people or the media, you can't escape the presentation of sex in today's society.

Questions

What triggers you into sexual temptations? Why?

_____
_____
_____
_____
_____
_____

How do you deal with sexual temptation (if you are dating someone answer from that point of view)?

_____
_____
_____
_____
_____
_____

Is it still a challenge or have you overcome it?

_____
_____
_____
_____
_____
_____

What do you constantly think about as a single person? Why?

_____
_____
_____
_____
_____
_____

Which of the three temptations of the mind do you struggle with?

_____
_____
_____
_____
_____
_____

How are you dealing with sexual thoughts?

_____
_____
_____
_____
_____

Let's Be Real about the Single Life

DEALING WITH LONELINESS

Let's Talk

What is your view of loneliness?

Dealing with Loneliness

Loneliness is a pain that we can do something about. Loneliness is an issue of intimacy. It often arises when something of very significant, intimate value is taken from us. It's a state of mind or feeling of being excluded from other people or God. Loneliness simply means to be alone. It's hard for many Christians to be alone, because we want love, acceptance and companionship. Many singles want all that, but from the opposite sex.

Questions

What is it that occupies your every thought? Why?

_____
_____
_____
_____
_____
_____

What significant losses of intimacy have you experienced?

_____
_____
_____
_____
_____
_____

What do you do when you get lonely?

_____
_____

_____
_____
_____
_____

Do you feel disconnected from others? Why?

_____
_____
_____
_____
_____
_____

Do you feel sad because there is no one else available to be with you?

_____
_____
_____
_____
_____
_____

Are you uncomfortable being alone?

_____
_____
_____
_____
_____

Do you feel abandoned? Why?

_____
_____
_____
_____
_____
_____

Do you feel left out? Why?

_____
_____
_____
_____
_____
_____

DATING

Let's Talk

Describe you perfect dating experience.

_____
_____
_____
_____
_____
_____
_____
_____
_____
_____
_____
_____
_____
_____
_____
_____
_____
_____
_____
_____

Dating

Dating is any social activity performed as a pair or even a group with the aim of each assessing the other's suitability as their partner in an intimate relationship or as a spouse. The word refers to the act of agreeing on a time and "date" when a pair can meet and engage in some social activity.

Most of the time when you're just dating, you're basically enjoying a buffet. You taste many items you want until you find what you like. I can relate to that. When I was in the world, I dated many different women with no intentions of settling down.

Questions

What is your view of dating? What is your view of courting?

_____
_____
_____
_____
_____
_____

What are you doing to become the right person for someone?

_____
_____
_____
_____
_____
_____

Have you set any boundaries? What are they?

_____
_____
_____
_____
_____

Are you really saving yourself for marriage?

_____
_____
_____
_____
_____

Are you dating like-minded/committed Christians? If no, why not?

_____
_____
_____
_____
_____

Do you have non-negotiable values? What are they?

_____
_____
_____
_____
_____
_____

Are you seeking God in your dating? If not, why?

_____
_____
_____
_____
_____
_____

Let's Be Real about the Single Life

THE 10 COMMANDMENTS OF DATING

Let's Talk

Why is it important to follow rules while dating?

The 10 Commandments of Dating

The one thing I had to realize was there was a process I had to go through before I could even be ready for a wife. And I had to realize that living single doesn't have to be as hard as we make it. Just as there are commandments given in the Bible to live by, there are certain dating principles needed in order to have a successful relationship.

Questions

What does honesty mean to you?

_____
_____
_____
_____
_____

Do you set boundaries in your relationships? What are they?

_____
_____
_____
_____
_____

What are some questions you ask in the beginning of a relationship? Do they five you any insight on the future of the relationship?

_____
_____
_____
_____
_____
_____

How do you feel about sex before marriage? Why?

_____
_____
_____
_____
_____
_____

What are some red flags that you see while dating?

_____
_____
_____
_____
_____
_____

What do you do when you see the red flags? Why?

_____
_____
_____
_____
_____

How do you feel about dating in groups? Why?

_____
_____
_____
_____
_____

Do you feel that you have settled in relationships? Are you settling now?

_____
_____
_____
_____
_____

How do you know when you are settling?

_____
_____
_____
_____
_____
_____

Do you make excuses for that person when you know they are not the one for you? Why?

_____
_____
_____
_____
_____
_____

Are you playing any games while dating? Why?

_____
_____
_____
_____
_____
_____

Are you with someone or interested in someone who is playing games?

_____
_____
_____
_____
_____
_____

What type of dating games have you experienced?

_____
_____
_____
_____
_____
_____

What dating games have you played on someone?

_____
_____
_____
_____
_____
_____

Are you open-minded in relationships?
_____
_____
_____
_____
_____
_____

Is the person you're dating or have dated open-minded?
_____
_____
_____
_____
_____
_____

Are you willing to try different things that the other person may like? If no, why not?
_____
_____
_____
_____
_____
_____

Have you given up something(s) that you were passionate about because the other person didn't like it? Why?

_____
_____
_____
_____
_____
_____

Do you generally take your time when dating?

_____
_____
_____
_____
_____
_____

Do you or have you used sex to determine compatibility? Why?

_____
_____
_____
_____
_____
_____

Why is your time is important?

_____
_____
_____
_____
_____
_____

Let's Be Real about the Single Life

BUILDING A SUCCESSFUL RELATIONSHIP

Let's Talk

What do you feel it takes to build a successful relationship?

_____
_____
_____
_____
_____
_____
_____
_____
_____
_____
_____
_____
_____
_____
_____
_____
_____
_____
_____
_____

Building a Successful Relationship

Marriage is a crucial subject among single Christians. I did a survey before writing this book, and everyone I surveyed said they wanted to be married. When talking about marriage, most singles think of just the ceremony and not about building a successful relationship that will build to a successful marriage. I myself thought that if I just found the right one, I would be ready. Now that I'm married, I've quickly learned it's more to it than that.

Questions

Why is building your personal foundation important?

_____
_____
_____
_____
_____
_____

To you, what does it mean to be financially stable?

_____
_____
_____
_____
_____
_____

What are you doing to become financially stable?

_____
_____
_____
_____
_____
_____

Are you emotionally stable? If no, why not?

_____
_____
_____
_____
_____
_____

How are you controlling you emotions?

_____
_____
_____
_____
_____
_____

What is the level of your spiritual stability?

_____
_____
_____
_____
_____
_____

Are you dating someone who is on another level spiritually? How does that make you feel?

_____
_____
_____
_____
_____
_____

Are you dating someone of another faith/religion? Why?

_____
_____
_____
_____
_____
_____

Do you immediately trust people? Why?

_____
_____
_____
_____
_____
_____

How do you develop trust in relationships?

_____
_____
_____
_____
_____
_____

How important is it to communicate your intentions in a relationship?

_____
_____
_____
_____
_____
_____

Do you do what you say you're going to do?

_____
_____
_____
_____
_____

When having a disagreement, do you try to see the other person's point of view? If no, why not?

_____
_____
_____
_____
_____

Do you always have to be right or have your own way? Why?

_____
_____
_____
_____
_____

How do you respond to criticism from the person you are dating?

_____
_____
_____
_____
_____
_____

Do you admit when you are wrong? If no, why not?

_____
_____
_____
_____
_____
_____

Which of the five relationship stages are you in right now? How do you know?

_____
_____
_____
_____
_____
_____

Let's Be Real about the Single Life

ARE YOU READY FOR MARRIAGE

Let's Talk

What is your viewpoint on marriage?

_____

"Are You Ready for Marriage?"

Is now the right time for you to get married? What do you need to know before you walk down the aisle? You should always want to take a closer look at yourself and the relationship before tying the knot. When I finally got focused on my life for real, I started to realize things about myself. At first I thought I was ready to be married.

But when I realized that I would have to take care of a wife and myself and put her needs before mine. It scared me a little, because I realized that I really wasn't ready for that commitment. When my wife and I were planning our wedding, we were not just planning for a day; we were planning for a lifetime.

Questions

Are You Ready for Marriage? How do you know?

_____
_____
_____
_____
_____

Have you built a stable personal foundation?

_____
_____
_____

_____
_____

Do you trust the person you are in a relationship with? If no, why

_____
_____
_____
_____
_____

Are you trustworthy? Explain.

_____
_____
_____
_____
_____

How is the communication in your relationship?

_____
_____
_____
_____
_____

Do you compromise with each other or must things always go your way?

_____
_____
_____
_____
_____
_____

Are you really ready to be married?

_____
_____
_____
_____
_____
_____

Why do you want to get married?

_____
_____
_____
_____
_____
_____

If engaged, why do you want to marry this person?

_____
_____
_____
_____
_____
_____

What are your expectations of your mate?

_____
_____
_____
_____
_____
_____

Do you have any reservations or doubts? If so, what are they?

_____
_____
_____
_____
_____
_____

Made in the USA
Lexington, KY
04 October 2014